Ephesians 3:20

"I am so grateful to God for the words sent to m
day waiting for the words of encouragement from
us daily to trust in God, and never give up on the vision that God ___
hearts. I am extremely proud of the possibility of her words blessing the lives of so
many others. I always knew that she was purposed to inspire the world, and I believe
that this is only the beginning!"

Judith A. Powell
Division leader- Future RVP Primerica Financial Services

"Ms. Ussin's book is the "go to" guide for how to encourage, inspire, and embolden
our families. I highly recommend it to everyone as a must read!"

Carmen J. Walters, PHD
President
Tougaloo College

"God uses Joyace so effectively in encouraging and reminding all of us of the power
and saving Grace of God's Word for our daily existence."

Emma Roberts
Friend and Neighbor
Retiree- Conoco Phillips

"Joyace (Lyn), you have taken an approach to leave your legacy behind in such beauty
and grace! I love this tool that you have developed to pour into young adults and
those who will be coming down the legacy pike. Many will be blessed, encouraged,
and gain nuggets for many years to come from the insight of these words of wisdom
and power. We need more positive spoken words that can reach the hearts of those
who will take things to the next level. Thanks for not just preaching another sermon,
but for pouring your heart and God's words in a way that others can warmly receive
them and in a way that their world can be changed.
May God continue to bless you in abundance!"

Elder Dr. Lynette Thompson Dandridge
Professor, Author, Knowledge Broker

"This body of work is a reminder that daily we have the renewed opportunity to
speak life into ourselves and into the lives of others. It is bound to incite some type
of growth and transformation. Readers are truly in for a treat."

LaToya Turner, MHA
Spiritual daughter and friend

THE POWER OF POSITIVE WORDS

AFFIRMATIONS FROM A MOTHER'S HEART

JOYACE G. USSIN

WestBow
PRESS®
A DIVISION OF THOMAS NELSON
& ZONDERVAN

WestBow Press books may be ordered through booksellers or by contacting:

WestBow Press
A Division of Thomas Nelson & Zondervan
1663 Liberty Drive
Bloomington, IN 47403
www.westbowpress.com
1 (866) 928-1240

Scripture taken from the King James Version of the Bible.

ISBN: 978-1-9736-7609-6 (sc)
ISBN: 978-1-9736-7610-2 (hc)
ISBN: 978-1-9736-7608-9 (e)

Library of Congress Control Number: 2019915165

Print information available on the last page.

WestBow Press rev. date: 11/12/2019

DEDICATION

To my adult children:

Lawrence (Ashley) Ussin Sr.

Judith (Derek) Powell Sr.

Alaina (Chao) Stevens

ACKNOWLEDGEMENTS

A special thanks to my husband of nearing 37 years, Lawrence Ussin Jr., for his love, patience and understanding throughout this process. Honey you are ALWAYS the strong silent force that keeps me moving.

To my beautiful children: Lawrence (Ashley), Judith (Derek) and Alaina (Chao), and their children, my grandchildren: Amari, Saniya, Talia, Derek Jr, Lawrence Jr, Kherington, and Marley, your futures are bright and unlimited; don't limit God and what He can do through you.

To my Dad, Charles Gibson, in my eyes you are totally, "Superman". Thank you for your love and strong work ethic that you have instilled in each one of us.

To my Mom, Joyace Donsereaux Gibson, I know that you are smiling down from Heaven. Thank you for always encouraging me and speaking life into every situation concerning me. I miss our talks.

To my bonus Mom, Yolanda, you have made all the difference in our Dad's life. Thank you for being there, you are a true blessing from God.

I would like to thank my awesome brothers: Charles, George, Wayne and Dwayne. You guys always step up in times of need.

To my beautiful in laws: Lawrence (deceased) and Lucille, your love for me has meant everything, and I am proud to call you my own.

To my sisters in law, and brother in law: Patricia, Denise, Pam, Vanessa, Diana, Mary, Lisa, Lupe, and Michael, God has a way of setting up and bringing families together. Thank you all for being that family which loves hard, laughs loud, and bonds tightly during good and hard times. I love you all.

To my dear friends and fellow authors, Toni Coleman-Carter and Linda Thompson, you ladies keep going and going and have always encouraged me to "get going".

To my "good" neighbors, Leroy and Emma Roberts, we, Lawrence and I, thank God everyday for the blessing that you two have been in our lives. You have made Texas a very welcoming place for us. Thank you!

To all of my girlfriends and Sisters in Christ, some new and some lifetime: Debra Johnson, Judith Pastor, Cynthia Smith, Rosemary Thomas, Danielle Mathis, Mary Wallace, Gladis Green, LaToya Turner, Kim Mobley, Twlia Martin, Juliette Reese, Belencia Breaux, and Maronda Chenault, thanks for being there and for enhancing my life. You all keep me on my toes... and knees. I love you to life!

To everyone I have encountered through the years that have taken my words to heart, and said, "You really should write a book!" Thank you; I finally took courage and put my words on paper.

Lastly and certainly not least, to the men that I have been privileged to call Pastors, who have poured into my life, watched over my soul, and directed me to Jesus and the Word of God for Life's answers: Pastor Rayford T. Iglehart; Prophet Robert Charles Blakes Sr (deceased); Pastor Leroy Phoenix Sr.; Pastor Christopher F. Hartwell, and Bishop RC Blakes Jr. Thank you all for being men of God that I can look up to. You are loved and appreciated.

FOREWORD

The Power of Positive Words is a multi-dimensional jewel. The author, Joyace Ussin, has a very quiet but profound prophetic mantle. In this work we get the very heart of Joyace as she gives us an open invitation into some of the most intimate and private interactions between she and her children. The Power of Positive Words is a collection of her morning declarations spoken over her adult children. You will sense the power of God!

You will feel the Spirit of God moving in your soul as you go through the daily process of reading the declarations; reviewing the corresponding scriptures; writing your takeaways, and pondering some very powerful quotes from some of the greatest minds.

This is a Spiritual jewel that will prove to help many find their way back to God and faith. It will also be an awesome aide to empower babes in beginning the process of meditation, as well as consecration. For those of us who are in sync spiritually, it will only serve to strengthen our resolve. Joyace has done an unbelievable job conveying her heart in a format that engages the reader while ministering to the soul and spirit.

RC Blakes, Jr.

INSTRUCTIONS ON USAGE OF
THIS DAILY DEVOTIONAL

The Power of Positive Words is a daily devotion tool that can positively impact your day; strengthen your prayer life, and your walk with the Lord, while depositing scripture into your spirit, when used properly.

Each morning, afternoon, or evening, whatever time you decide to devote to communicating with the Lord, begin by reading the positive affirmation of the day. Then repeat the simple prayer out loud. You can enhance or personalize the prayer to whatever your need from the Lord is for the day. Lastly, take a few moments to read each scripture reference (which is conveniently located in the back of this devotional book), meditate on the Word of God and commit the scripture to memory.

A journal page has been provided for each day, and at the end of your bonus days, so that you will have an opportunity to write your thoughts, reflections or revelations, for the day, while being encouraged by a positive quote near the end of each page.

If used properly this little devotional will not only enhance your prayer life, your love for and commitment to God, but also your pathway to success. A true relationship with God is the beginning of a positive existence, and my prayer is that *The Power of Positive Words* will assist you in deepening your relationship with the Lord.

INTRODUCTION

I once heard a preacher speak of an old Greek fable wherein a god asked another god to present the worst gift in the world. The next day that god came back with a box. On the inside of the box was a tongue. Then the god asked the other god to present the best gift in the world. The next day that god came back again with a box. On the inside of the box was a tongue. That is right! The tongue can be the worst gift and the best gift! Proverbs 18:21 says, "Death and life *are* in the power of the tongue: and they that love it shall eat the fruit thereof." I have known this scripture for years and had never truly related it in this manner. On that day I decided that EVERYDAY that the Lord allows me to live that I would speak positive affirmations to bring life to my children! My prayer is that these affirmations would not only influence them but also transfer to everyone that they come into contact with. Having been called to preach the Gospel of Jesus Christ, it is easy to find fault, and begin to preach to your children about shortcomings or disappointments; however, I found that eventually they do not hear you anymore. Consequently, they begin to resent the God of their Salvation. How unfortunate it would be for people everywhere to receive God's Word and blessings through you, and your own children cannot stand to hear your voice! I thank God that He revealed this truth to me before we got to that point, but make no mistake, I was on a train moving at warp speed in that direction. Therefore, I thank God that I can still hear His voice, and that I was obedient. This made me began to listen to my own words: pause, reflect, and think before I would even speak to my adult children about the way that I felt they were mishandling life and its affairs. My husband and I are always discussing how we raised our children in the fear of the Lord, and how, now, we MUST trust the God that we know dwells richly in them. He, Lawrence, is always that calm voice of reason when I am ready to pull out the sword and just start wrecking things. I thank God everyday for the E.F. Hutton of our family, because when he speaks, we all listen. Therefore, through the encouragement of my husband, children and a few others, I decided to put these affirmations in print form so that other young adults or even older adults could benefit from *The Power of Positive Words*. I send a daily text message to my children and the next several pages are the actual messages that they received on a daily basis. I have added scripture and a prayer for meditation purposes. I know that if used daily these words, scriptures, and prayers will make a difference in how the reader thinks and feels about each day that the Lord Jesus allows them to enjoy. All Glory belongs to God!

DAY ONE

You are Strong! You are Courageous! You are Confident! You are Powerful! You can accomplish anything that you set your mind to. You were born for greatness. Don't doubt yourself or live beneath your potential. You are a WINNER, and I am very proud of you.

> #doubtanddowithout
> #believeandrecieve

PRAYER:

Lord, I know that I cannot do anything on my own, but by Your strength I can do all things. Help me today to be my best, and to overcome the things that I have feared in the past. I am confident that You are with me because You promised never to leave me. I will put my trust in You Lord. In Jesus' name I pray. Amen.

SCRIPTURE:

> Mark 11:24
> Philippians 4:13
> John 14:18

My Reflections and Revelations

_____
_____
_____
_____
_____
_____
_____
_____
_____
_____
_____
_____
_____
_____
_____
_____
_____
_____
_____
_____
_____
_____

"

"Smile, It's free therapy" –Douglas Horton

"

DAY TWO

Just as the sun rises every morning, the SON rises in you! Greater is He that is in you than he that is in the World! You belong to God, and He will give you GRACE to accomplish what He has ordained for your life! Seek Him, the Lord Jesus, for direction EVERYDAY! And like Visa, don't leave home without Him!

#HeisbetterthanVisa

PRAYER:

Father God, in the name of Jesus, I ask that Your light shine through me on today. Guide me by Your Holy Spirit so that I may accomplish everything that You have planned for my life, and allow my life to bring Glory to You! Shield me from evil, and go before me as You promised. This I pray in Jesus' name. Amen.

SCRIPTURE:

I John 4:4b
Deuteronomy 31:8
Matthew 6:33

My Reflections and Revelations

_____
_____
_____
_____
_____
_____
_____
_____
_____
_____
_____
_____
_____
_____
_____
_____
_____
_____
_____
_____
_____
_____

66 ——————————————————————————

"Motivation is what gets you started. Habit
is what keeps you going" -Jim Ryun

—————————————————————————— 99

DAY THREE

Yesterday is past. Tomorrow is coming. Today is present, and you are the gift that God is presenting to the World! Use your talents, strengths, power, as well as weaknesses, to Glorify HIM!

#youarefearfullyandwonderfullymade

PRAYER:

Heavenly Father, forgive me for not presenting my best self everyday and in every way. Thank You for every challenge, test, trial and victory. I know that because of Your love, mercy, and grace I am given new opportunities every day. Use me for Your Glory Lord! In Jesus' name I pray. Amen.

SCRIPTURE:

Lamentations 3:22-23
Psalms 139:14
Psalms 119:77

My Reflections and Revelations

_____
_____
_____
_____
_____
_____
_____
_____
_____
_____
_____
_____
_____
_____
_____
_____
_____
_____
_____
_____
_____

66

"Someday everything will make perfect sense. So, for now, laugh at the confusion, smile through the tears, and keep reminding yourself that everything happens for a reason." -Unknown

99

DAY FOUR

As the days come and go, so will challenges, disappointments, as well as Victories. Get up and face each day knowing that YOU are MORE THAN A CONQUEROR; and if God has allowed you to see the day, then HE is not through using or blessing you! YOU ARE A VESSEL WORTHY OF USING! NOW, GO FORTH!

#yougotthis

PRAYER:

Father God, thank You for another day. A day I have not seen before. A day of new beginnings. A day filled with new mercies to produce all that You, Lord, desire for my life. Thank You for health, strength and power to face this day with full expectation that great things are in store for me. Thank You for going before me and preparing all things for my success. This I pray in Jesus' name. Amen.

SCRIPTURE:

Psalms 103:4
Deuteronomy 31:8
Romans 8:37

My Reflections and Revelations

_____
_____
_____
_____
_____
_____
_____
_____
_____
_____
_____
_____
_____
_____
_____
_____
_____
_____
_____
_____
_____

66 ———————————————————————————

*"Remember, you can't reach what's in front of you until
you let go of what's behind you." -Unknown*

——————————————————————— 99

DAY FIVE

I know that this scripture has been used over and over to encourage folks to keep going: "I can do all things through Christ who strengthens me" (Philippians 4:13). However, this applies when things are not going well. Paul learned that whether I am doing poorly or well, I can still survive. YOU can survive! YOU can do ALL things as Christ gives you strength!

#reallifeishappening

PRAYER:

Father God, thank You for strength to face every day. The days that I am disappointed, I know that You guide me. The days that I am full of joy, I know You balance me. And the days I just cannot seem to go on, I know that You love me. I know that I can do all things as You give me strength. In Jesus name I pray. Amen

SCRIPTURE:

Philippians 4:13
Ephesians 6:11
Proverbs 3:6

My Reflections and Revelations

_____

_____

_____

_____

_____

_____

_____

_____

_____

_____

_____

_____

_____

_____

_____

_____

_____

_____

_____

❝

*"A man is what he thinks about all day
long." –Ralph Waldo Emerson*

❞

DAY SIX

The second that YOU realize that you are living beneath your potential, things will begin to change! A made up mind, determination, preparation, and education open opportunities to become successful!! DO YOUR HOMEWORK!! BE PREPARED!! SAY YOUR PRAYERS, then TAKE THE TEST!! NOBODY can do it for you. It WILL be HARD, however YOU CAN DO IT!! Every success story has a beginning!! P.S. there will ALWAYS be something to cry about, but make LAUGHTER your release! Water coupled with sunshine causes growth!

#Godiswithyou

PRAYER:

Father God, thank You for this day even with all of the test and hardships. I know and understand that there is great potential in me to accomplish everything that You have purposed for my life. I look to You for strength, peace and joy. I know you are with me. In Jesus name I pray. Amen.

SCRIPTURES:

Proverbs 9:10
Philippians 4:13
Philippians 2:5

My Reflections and Revelations

_____

_____

_____

_____

_____

_____

_____

_____

_____

_____

_____

_____

_____

_____

_____

_____

_____

_____

_____

66

"Life has no limitations, except the ones you make." –Les Brown

99

DAY SEVEN

Don't allow other people's opinions, doubts, and insecurities dampen your God given inspirations! Even though Jesus knew he was going to be betrayed and crucified He remained true to the purpose that God created Him for. Even if you make several mistakes, get up each time believing in yourself and the God of your salvation!

#stayfocused

PRAYER:

Father God, forgive me for not trusting You enough to walk into my destiny. When I am weak, I can count on You to strengthen me. Help me to see myself as You see me. Help me to know that I am on the path that You chose for my life. Give me courage and wisdom to live out Your purpose for my life; for I know that You are with me. In Jesus' name I pray. Amen.

SCRIPTURE:

Proverbs 3:4–5
John 14:16
Psalms 55:17

My Reflections and Revelations

_____
_____
_____
_____
_____
_____
_____
_____
_____
_____
_____
_____
_____
_____
_____
_____
_____
_____
_____
_____
_____
_____

" "

"Sometimes you need to quit the mediocre things to experience the AMAZING things." -Unknown

DAY EIGHT

2018 Winter Olympics Women's Cross Country Race... the U.S. Olympian fell in first lap. She got up, took a deep breath and skied full speed ahead for 90 minutes. She climbed up, down, and around. She FINISHED the course in seventh place. YOU may be facing a hard course in this season of your life; don't fret! If you fall, GET UP! TAKE A DEEP BREATH, EVALUATE WHERE YOU ARE, then GET MOVING AGAIN!! FINISH THE COURSE!! Seven is the number of completion! I believe that Olympian, who trained for 4 years just to qualify for the race, will NEVER place seventh again. Learn and grow from EVERY adventure. GREATNESS RESIDES IN YOU!

#dontquitFINISH!!

PRAYER:

Father God, I have tried so many things in life and it seems as though I am failing or cannot find the courage to finish what I started. Please Lord help me to see the ending from the beginning, and increase my strength as the journey gets hard. I know that if I continue to trust You that there is nothing that I cannot do. In Jesus name I pray. Amen.

SCRIPTURE:

Philippians 1:6
Ecclesiastics 9:11
Proverbs 3:5

My Reflections and Revelations

_____
_____
_____
_____
_____
_____
_____
_____
_____
_____
_____
_____
_____
_____
_____
_____
_____
_____
_____
_____

66

"The only way to make sense out of change is to plunge into it, move with it, and join the dance." Alan Watts

99

DAY NINE

I know, I REALLY know, that there are times that you wished that you had done or said or even acted differently. Some days you are reminded of past failures or missed opportunities. The GOOD NEWS is… THAT'S the past!! Even if it were just yesterday, it's all behind you. NOW, adjust the rear view mirror and look FORWARD through that LARGE window in front of you. Adorn your glasses if you need to. But see CLEARLY ALL of the opportunities ahead!! YOUR BEST DAYS ARE YET TO COME and I am so very proud of you! When I look at all of you, I see: Entrepreneurs, Artist, Musicians, Writers, Organizers, and Financiers!

#stronglegacy
#MAKEITGREAT

PRAYER:

Father God, thank You for the greatness that You created in me even before I was born. Thank You for helping me to reach that potential, and allowing others to see Your Glory in it. Help me to remain humble as You exalt me. In Jesus name I pray. Amen

SCRIPTURE:

Psalms 29:1
Jeremiah 29:11
Philippians 4:7

My Reflections and Revelations

_____
_____
_____
_____
_____
_____
_____
_____
_____
_____
_____
_____
_____
_____
_____
_____
_____
_____
_____
_____

66 ——————————————————————————

"Not everything that is faced can be changed, but nothing can be changed until it is faced." –James Baldwin

————————————————————————— 99

DAY TEN

You have heard the expression, "BETTER LATE THAN NEVER", right? Well it does not matter what circumstances look like, JUST GET STARTED! Begin working towards your goals. Make a Vision Board or keep a notepad close with checklists and inspirational thoughts that will thrust you towards your purposeful destination. God has given you the tools and talent. He placed your destiny in your hands. He told you to write the vision and make it plain. He told you to meditate on the Word. RUN TOWARDS THE VISION!

#destinyiswaitingonyou!

PRAYER:

Father God, I know that You are the author and finisher of my faith. Thank You that You know my name and have placed greatness on the inside of me. Thank You for giving me Your vision for my life, and the strength to move towards it. I know I will see Your Glory in my life and others will be blessed because of it. In Jesus' name I pray. Amen.

SCRIPTURES:

Hebrews 12:2
Habakkuk 2:2
I John 4:4

My Reflections and Revelations

_____

_____

_____

_____

_____

_____

_____

_____

_____

_____

_____

_____

_____

_____

_____

_____

_____

_____

_____

_____

_____

" ——————————————————————

_"You must do the thing that you think you
cannot do." —Eleanor Roosevelt_

———————————————————— **"**

DAY ELEVEN

You were created to DOMINATE AND SUBDUE! If you want God's finest, YOU MUST give Him your best. Stop making excuses for why you can't and start rejoicing in what you can do. God honors those who honor Him. Rise, pray, prepare and GO FORTH!!

#GREATNESSRESIDESINYOU
#PUTGODFIRST

PRAYER:

Father God, forgive me for putting off what You have purposed me to do. I can no longer deny why I was created. Please help my unbelief as I venture forward in completing what You have started in me. In Jesus' name I pray. Amen

SCRIPTURE:

Gen 1:26-28
Mark 9:24
Romans 8:28

My Reflections and Revelations

_____
_____
_____
_____
_____
_____
_____
_____
_____
_____
_____
_____
_____
_____
_____
_____
_____
_____
_____

66

"If we as a people realized the greatness from which we came we would be less likely to disrespect ourselves." -Marcus Garvey

99

DAY TWELVE

BAM! Sometimes reality and life hits so hard it can feel like a sucker punch that you neither saw nor discerned was heading your way. It can literally knock the wind out of your sails. Nevertheless, be encouraged because Jesus said that in this life you would have tribulations, "BUT I HAVE OVERCOME THE WORLD"! Stand, for you can overcome your trials because He has made you an overcomer. Therefore, look to the hills, where your help comes from. Because "greater is He that is in you, than he that is in the world! (John 4:4) Trust Him!!

#greaterresidesinyou

PRAYER:

Father God, thank You for always going before me to make crooked paths straight. I know that You have already predestined my success. Help me to stand even in the face of adversity, knowing that the victory is mine. In Jesus' mighty name, I pray. Amen.

SCRIPTURE:

John 16:33
Psalms 121:1-2
Isaiah 45:2

My Reflections and Revelations

_____

_____

_____

_____

_____

_____

_____

_____

_____

_____

_____

_____

_____

_____

_____

_____

_____

_____

_____

_____

_____

_____

66

"You cannot cross the sea merely by standing and staring at the water." –Rabindranath Tagore

99

DAY THIRTEEN

You are CONFIDENT, BOLD, STRONG, BEAUTIFUL, and SUCCESSFUL! You will be very productive today and the tears you have sown will reap a harvest of JOY, PEACE and FINANCIAL BLESSINGS!! Put on the full armor of God so that you will be able to stand against the attacks of the enemy. All of the schemes plots and plans that the enemy had to destroy your life will be cancelled!

> #Godsworkingitout
> #Goodforevil
> #lightinthedarkness

PRAYER:

Father God, thank You for allowing me to be all that You have created me to be. I know that in You I have everything that I need, and that all things are provided through You. I stand today fully equipped in your Word, and I know that nothing will stop the purpose that You have for my life. In Jesus' name I pray. Amen.

SCRIPTURE:

> Ephesians 6:11-18
> Isaiah 54:17
> John 1:5

My Reflections and Revelations

_____
_____
_____
_____
_____
_____
_____
_____
_____
_____
_____
_____
_____
_____
_____
_____
_____
_____
_____
_____
_____
_____

66 ————————————————————————————

*"You can, you should, and if you're brave enough
to start, you will."* —Stephen King

——————————————————————— 99

DAY FOURTEEN

WORDS!! The WORD! Your word! Words create! Everything that is, was created by THE WORD. YOU have the power to create life or death with your words. You were created in God's image and HIS likeness. THINK about what you are going to say, then SPEAK WHAT YOU WANT TO SEE! Because your words WILL come to pass!

#itsinyourmouth
#speakwhatyouwanttosee

PRAYER:

Father God, help me to control my own mouth. I understand the power that is in the spoken word because of how You created me. Teach me to speak and expect manifestation without doubting. In Jesus' name I pray. Amen

SCRIPTURE:

Ephesians 3:20
Proverbs 18:21
Psalms 19:14

My Reflections and Revelations

_____

_____

_____

_____

_____

_____

_____

_____

_____

_____

_____

_____

_____

_____

_____

_____

_____

_____

_____

_____

_____

66

"The best is yet to be." – Robert Browning

99

DAY FIFTEEN

WORDS!! The Bible says that "you are snared (trapped, committed) by the words of your mouth". Consider your words before you speak them. Don't commit or say you are going to do something unless you mean it. If you commit then follow through. My Momma always said, "Your word is your bond (verbal contract)".

> #keepyourword
> #nomoreexcuses

PRAYER:

Father God, help me to think before I speak words that will not be productive for my life. Give me the strength to commit and do the things that I have spoken out of my mouth. Let my words be honorable. In Jesus' name I pray. Amen.

SCRIPTURE:

> Proverbs 6:2
> Romans 4:17
> Psalms 10:14

My Reflections and Revelations

_____
_____
_____
_____
_____
_____
_____
_____
_____
_____
_____
_____
_____
_____
_____
_____
_____
_____
_____
_____
_____

“

"A problem is a chance for you to do your best." –Duke Ellington

”

DAY SIXTEEN

JOY is a simple word that encompasses a large range of emotion. You may experience it whether you are expecting it or not. It is that feeling at the birth of a baby; of the successful completion of a hard task; of recovery from illness, or of seeing a loved one that you have not seen in a while. Praying that you will experience countless hours of joy! Joy can be present even in times of despair. It's the substance of strength. The Joy of the Lord is our strength!

> #seekjoyknowstrength
> #joyinservinghim

PRAYER:

Heavenly Father, thank You for joy unspeakable! Thank You for the strength that comes from just knowing You. As I seek You I know that everything that I need will be added to my life. In You my life is embedded. In Jesus' name I pray. Amen.

SCRIPTURE:

> Nehemiah 8:10
> Matt 6:33
> Acts 17:28

My Reflections and Revelations

_____

_____

_____

_____

_____

_____

_____

_____

_____

_____

_____

_____

_____

_____

_____

_____

_____

_____

_____

_____

_____

❝

"The most important thing is to look ahead. The past is your anchor." —Maxime Lagace'

❞

DAY SEVENTEEN

At the end of the day, YOU make sure that YOU can look YOURSELF in the face knowing that YOU did YOUR best. Whether building a business or reputation, NOTHING duplicates HARD WORK AND HONESTY. YOU CAN be successful at ALL LEVELS! Be accountable, first to God, then to yourself and others.

> #welldone
> #towhommuchisgivenmuchisrequired

PRAYER:

Father God, forgive me for not always seeking You first before making moves. I understand that if I am faithful in the few things that You have provided, it is then that I can expect more. Help me to continue to be honest and accountable in all that I do. In Jesus' name I pray. Amen.

SCRIPTURE:

> Matthew 6:33
> Matthew 25:23
> James 1:23

My Reflections and Revelations

_____
_____
_____
_____
_____
_____
_____
_____
_____
_____
_____
_____
_____
_____
_____
_____
_____
_____

66

"One small positive thought can change
your whole day." – Zig Ziglar

99

DAY EIGHTEEN

Negative thoughts, images and words will come but YOU have the power to dismiss them! The weapons that God has given you can create Victories! "For the weapons of our warfare are not carnal but Mighty through God to the pulling down of strongholds. Casting down all imaginations and bringing every thought under subjection of Jesus Christ." (II Corinthians 10:4-5). Change your words, thoughts, and images, and YOU CAN change your world!!

#YOUareaworldchanger!

PRAYER:

Father, God, thank You for giving me the tools and capacity to change through the power of your Holy Spirit and Word. Help me each day to seek You constantly for direction; and to listen intently for instruction for success. I know that nothing that is accomplished can be accomplished without Your divine intervention. In Jesus' name I pray, Amen.

SCRIPTURE:

Philippians 4:8
Proverbs 3:5-6
Zechariah 4:6

My Reflections and Revelations

_____

_____

_____

_____

_____

_____

_____

_____

_____

_____

_____

_____

_____

_____

_____

_____

_____

_____

_____

_____

_____

_____

"

"Joy is not in things; it is in us." –Richard Wagner

"

DAY NINETEEN

How many days have passed since you said, "I am going to do this or that?" Procrastination is a destroyer of Destiny! The only thing that comes to a sleeper is a dream! YOU have some exposed, as well as, hidden talents and gifts that are unused or being put on the back burner. Choose the path you want to follow. WRITE your vision (what YOU want to see come to pass in your life and future); READ it daily for motivation; SPEAK out loud to change the atmosphere, so that you can hear it and get it deep into your spirit; MOVE in the direction you desire to see the change, and WATCH God bring it to pass!

#yourdestinyiswaitingonyou

PRAYER:

Heavenly Father, forgive me for wasting the precious time that You have allowed in my life. Please help me to hear Your voice concerning how to begin and complete Your purpose in my life, and to reach my preordained destiny. Help me to recognize persons that are assigned to my life and to stop wasting time with destiny robbers and blockers. In Jesus' name I pray, Amen.

SCRIPTURE:

Ecclesiastes 3:11
II Corinthians 6:2
Psalm 90:12

My Reflections and Revelations

_____

_____

_____

_____

_____

_____

_____

_____

_____

_____

_____

_____

_____

_____

_____

_____

_____

_____

_____

"

"There is no promise without process" -RC Blakes Jr

"

DAY TWENTY

If EVERYTHING in your life is going well, then you are too compliant to the status quo! Don't be MEDIOCRE! To reign in EXCELLENCE you WILL BE challenged DAILY! Put on your armour and STAY in the fight!

#thebattleisnotyours
#getmoving

PRAYER:

Father God, forgive me for becoming a statistic, in that I have yielded to being just like everyone else. Lord, help me to be the unique individual that You created with gifts and talents that can and will glorify You. Help me to be strong and courageous whenever times are hard and I cannot see any resolve. Lord, help me to stand knowing that You already have my future secured. In Jesus' name I pray, Amen.

SCRIPTURES:

I Peter 5:7
Isaiah 41:13
Psalm 27:1

My Reflections and Revelations

"

"Beauty begins the moment you decide
to be yourself." —Coco Chanel

"

DAY TWENTY-ONE

Crises create moments of truth and trust. During a crisis you learn who is truthful and in whom you can trust. PUT YOUR TRUST IN GOD! And the truth you will find is that HE IS a very present help in a time of need. Stop telling EVERYONE your problems and start telling the ONLY ONE that can do ANYTHING about EVERYTHING! HE hears you! And HE WILL answer!

#HEisanONTIMEGOD

PRAYER:

Father God, I call upon and cry out to You this day because I know that You are the only one in whom I can truly trust. You are the one I can depend upon to help me in this current situation. I am running boldly to You asking for help in my time of need so that I can obtain your grace and mercy. I know that I will find strength and comfort in You. In Jesus' name I pray, Amen.

SCRIPTURE:

Hebrews 4:16
Proverbs 16:3
Psalm 143:8

My Reflections and Revelations

_____

_____

_____

_____

_____

_____

_____

_____

_____

_____

_____

_____

_____

_____

_____

_____

_____

_____

_____

_____

❝

"Live as if your prayers are to be answered." -Unknown

❞

DAY TWENTY-TWO

PROCRASTINATION, DISTRACTIONS, DETOURS, BAD DECISIONS! All of the above can be reasons to quit or not even get started. So you messed up; waited too long, or made a bad decision. What's done is DONE! Wipe the slate clean! Each new day is a NEW OPPORTUNITY to begin again! Take a deep breath. Get a good night's sleep. Make a good assessment of what you did right, and what went wrong. Then GET BACK TO WORK! ALWAYS, ALWAYS remember JESUS!! And you will be just fine. The only true failure is NEVER TRYING!

#thirdforthorevenfifthtimeisacharm

PRAYER:

Father God, I have messed up again! Forgive me Lord for all and any transgressions. I repent now in Jesus' mighty name. Lord, I know that if I keep my eyes on You, and my heart tuned into your Spirit that I can succeed at whatever it is You are directing me through. Please give me favor and the courage to move forward. This I pray in Jesus' name. Amen.

SCRIPTURE:

I John 5:14
Psalm 62:7
Psalm 145:18

My Reflections and Revelations

_____

_____

_____

_____

_____

_____

_____

_____

_____

_____

_____

_____

_____

_____

_____

_____

_____

_____

_____

_____

66 ————————————————————————

"Positive anything is better than negative nothing." –Elbert Hubbard

———————————————————— 99

DAY TWENTY-THREE

Embrace differences! People and cultures are true educators in life. Knowledge adds value, and all education does not come from books. Keep an open mind to listening, hearing, and discussing things that you are not necessarily familiar with. Exploration heightens your existence! Be flexible, while holding true to morals!

> #youarevaluable
> #upgradelifeexperinces

PRAYER:

Father God, in the name of Jesus, please help me to stand in this new arena that You have allowed me to enter. Give me wisdom daily on how to maneuver and become successful in this venture. Let Your glory shine through me as I witness through my work ethic and conversation regarding Your goodness and mercy. Help me to be all that You have created me to be. In Jesus' name I pray, Amen.

SCRIPTURE:

> Proverbs 16:20
> Psalm 31:19
> James 1:5

My Reflections and Revelations

_____

_____

_____

_____

_____

_____

_____

_____

_____

_____

_____

_____

_____

_____

_____

_____

_____

_____

_____

_____

_____

66

"Be the light in the dark, be the calm in the storm and be at peace while at war." —Mike Dolan

99

DAY TWENTY-FOUR

Some days, "it's just like that!" No matter what you do, or how positive you think or speak, STUFF HAPPENS! On those days, SEEK GOD! LOOK FOR GOOD IN EVERY SITUATION! MEDITATE ON GOD'S WORD! And KEEP IT MOVING!! At the end of the day, you will be delighted at how much you REALLY did accomplish through the influence of keeping a productive mindset!

#stayfocusedvictoryisnear

PRAYER:

Father God, I did not see this disappointment coming. Thank You for keeping me in the midst of it all. Thank You for allowing me to stay focused on Your goodness, and not be devoured by the circumstances. Thank You for Your faithfulness to Your Word, and for the promise that You would always be with me. Because of You, I can go on. In Jesus' name I pray, Amen.

SCRIPTURE:

Acts 17:27
Hebrews 11:6
James 4:8

My Reflections and Revelations

_____
_____
_____
_____
_____
_____
_____
_____
_____
_____
_____
_____
_____
_____
_____
_____
_____
_____
_____
_____

❝

*"There are far, far better things ahead than
anything we leave behind." —C.S. Lewis*

❞

DAY TWENTY-FIVE

Celebrate EVERYDAY as if it were your birthday! Every day is a new beginning. Every day brings new opportunities; new mercies; new favor; new Grace, but SAME GOD! The One who can and will make a difference! Trust Him! He sees you right where you are. MORE is working for you in the unseen than in the seen!

#keepitmoving

PRAYER:

Father God, thank You for a new day, new mercies and favor. Thank You for never changing, and always being the truth in my life. Help me to celebrate in this life all that You have done, are doing, and will do in and through me. Thank You for protecting and providing for me. In Jesus' name I pray, Amen.

SCRIPTURE:

Lamentations 3:22-23
Hebrews 13:8
Philippians 4:19

My Reflections and Revelations

_____
_____
_____
_____
_____
_____
_____
_____
_____
_____
_____
_____
_____
_____
_____
_____
_____
_____
_____

"

"Most of the important things in the world have been accomplished by people who have kept on trying when there seemed to be no hope at all." –Dale Carnegie

"

DAY TWENTY-SIX

Prayer gets God's attention. Praise opens up heaven for blessings to form. Worship causes blessings to fall down. What position are you in? I believe that your blessings are on the way once you assume the correct position. Don't wait....Pray, Praise, and Worship because this battle is not yours, it is the Lord's!

#itsinyourmouth

PRAYER:

O Lord, how I praise and worship You! I thank You for every breath that You allow. Thank You for all of your provision for me and my loved ones. Thank You for the desire to worship you in spirit and truth. Father, I am desperate for a deeper fellowship with You, because I realize that in You my joy will be completely fulfilled. Forgive me so that I can bask in Your presence. This I pray in Jesus' name, Amen.

SCRIPTURE:

Psalm 103:1
Psalm 16:11
John 4:24

My Reflections and Revelations

_____

_____

_____

_____

_____

_____

_____

_____

_____

_____

_____

_____

_____

_____

_____

_____

_____

_____

_____

66

> *"**I AM** is everything that you need Him to be.*
> *Position yourself for blessings! Joyace G. Ussin*

DAY TWENTY-SEVEN

Silence! It is in the silence that we learn to listen and trust! Trust God in the hard times, even when you cannot hear anything. For God says that He will be with you on the mountaintops and definitely in the valleys. He will not forget about you. At the appointed time (the time that He has ordained), He will lift you up. You are WINNING, even when it doesn't feel like it!

#Godisnotdead

PRAYER:

Father God, help me to stand on what I already know of You and not be moved by what I see. Give me the courage to move forward to completion of the assignment I was given when I last heard Your instruction. I know that You have an appointed time for every aspect of my life. Please help me to wait on you when I need to. These prayers I pray in Jesus' name, Amen.

SCRIPTURE:

Genesis 18:14
Isaiah 41:10
Jeremiah 29:11

My Reflections and Revelations

---

66 —————————————————————————

"We must embrace pain and burn it as fuel
for our journey." —Kenji Miyazawa

————————————————————————— 99

DAY TWENTY-EIGHT

Praise! Thanksgiving! Worship! Start your day off being grateful for whatever it is that you already have. Whether it is in abundance or lack at the moment. Let your Heavenly Father know that you appreciate the life that HE has allowed to exist in you! Every time your soul (mind, will, emotions) wants to grumble and complain, remember the sacrifice that Jesus made so that you can gain a relationship with the Father. Nothing happens by accident! God has a journey mapped out for each of our lives, and no matter how far we travel away....ALL roads lead back to Him, when we accept His plan for our lives. LIVE for Him, because He DIED for YOU!

> #Heslookingforavessel
> #LetHimuseyou

PRAYER:

Father God I surrender all to You. Forgive me for not trusting You during my hardest times. I know that I can come boldly to Your throne during my time of need. I can call upon You and You will answer and show me great things that I cannot even imagine. Thank You Father because You have secured my future as I live for You. This I pray in Jesus' name. Amen.

SCRIPTURE:

> Jeremiah 33:3
> Proverbs 3:5
> Hebrews 4:16

My Reflections and Revelations

_____
_____
_____
_____
_____
_____
_____
_____
_____
_____
_____
_____
_____
_____
_____
_____
_____
_____
_____
_____

❝

*"Little minds are tamed and subdued by misfortune; but
great minds rise above them." —Washington Irving*

❞

DAY TWENTY-NINE

Early morning begins a new day! God is Faithful! He allowed the sun to rise again, just as He allowed you to rise. Now SHINE! Use all of the gifts and talents that He has bestowed you with. All He wants is for you to remember HIM in ALL that you do. Ask Him today, "Lord, what can I do for you today?" Sit still for a while and He will answer!

#listenforHisvoice
#youareaninstrument
#letHimuseyoutoday

PRAYER:

Father God, thank You for every day that You allow me to live. Help me to let my light shine so that men will see my good works and glorify You. Lord I am available to You, and am willing to do whatever You need me to do. Help me to be obedient to Your will and way. In Jesus' name I pray. Amen.

SCRIPTURE:

Matthew 5:16
Ephesians 2:10
Deuteronomy 11:1

My Reflections and Revelations

_____
_____
_____
_____
_____
_____
_____
_____
_____
_____
_____
_____
_____
_____
_____
_____
_____
_____
_____
_____

66

*"Think big thoughts but relish small
pleasures." –H. Jackson Brown*

99

DAY THIRTY

Hallelujah! Jesus is Alive!! Because He lives you can live eternally! He opened a true avenue for a full relationship with the Father. The veil was torn and we can enter into His presence! Find time to seek Him daily. Seeking Him will make a difference. Jesus ALWAYS does!

> #Heisnear
> #enterin

PRAYER:

Father God, forgive me for not always looking to You and seeking Your presence. Thank You for allowing Jesus to die on my behalf, which allowed for my access to eternal life. Lord I want to thank You for the privilege of entering into Your presence where I can find grace and mercy. In Jesus' name I pray. Amen.

SCRIPTURE:

> Isaiah 55:6
> Matthew 27:51
> Hebrews 4:16

My Reflections and Revelations

_____
_____
_____
_____
_____
_____
_____
_____
_____
_____
_____
_____
_____
_____
_____
_____
_____
_____
_____
_____
_____
_____
_____

66 —————————————————————————

"Keep your face to the sunshine and you
cannot see a shadow." – Helen Keller

————————————————————————— 99

DAY THIRTY-ONE

Your decisions or choices can be stepping stones or stumbling blocks. Make a decision to always do the right thing. Your choice may not always feel good or be popular, but if you allow the Spirit to guide you, this will always be the best decision for your life. LISTEN for His voice! It will be those goose bumps or hairs standing up on the back of your neck; that little twinge in your gut, or that very small inner voice saying, "Stop, take a minute" or "don't do that!"

#Godisnear
#Hesalwaysspeaking

PRAYER:

Father God, help me through Your Holy Spirit to hear Your voice and make the right decisions in life. Lead me through Your Word in the direction that You desire. Help me not to stray for selfish gain or ambition. This I pray in Jesus' name. Amen.

SCRIPTURES:

Psalms 119:105
Proverbs 3:6-7
I Kings 19:12

My Reflections and Revelations

_____

_____

_____

_____

_____

_____

_____

_____

_____

_____

_____

_____

_____

_____

_____

_____

_____

_____

❝

*"You can't control what's happening, challenge yourself
to control the way you respond to what's happening.
That's where your power is!"- Unknown*

❞

BONUS DAYS

DAY ONE

Responsibilities, wouldn't life be awesome if we didn't have them? NO, because we would have no motivation to dream, pursue or establish goals! Stop viewing responsibilities as a burden, and begin to count them as blessings! It is a blessing to have a roof over your head! It is a blessing to have a decent automobile! It is a blessing to prepare a good meal and to be able to eat a few times a day! It is a blessing to have a job that pays for your services! It is a blessing to have children who look to you for security! It is a blessing to have clothes to wear! It is a blessing to be a part of a family! It is a blessing to have talents and skills that you can use on a daily basis! Stop Whining and start WINNING! You are blessed!

> #stayfocused
> #keepitmoving
> #youaremorethanaconquerer

PRAYER:

Father God, thank You for every blessing that You have bestowed upon my life. Forgive me for whining and complaining about things that do not matter. I appreciate Your love and sacrifice so that I can have abundant life. In Jesus' name I pray. Amen.

SCRIPTURES:

> Deuteronomy 28:3-5
> Proverbs 16:3
> John 10:10

My Reflections and Revelations

_____
_____
_____
_____
_____
_____
_____
_____
_____
_____
_____
_____
_____
_____
_____
_____
_____
_____
_____
_____

66

"Write it on your heart that every day is the best day of the year." - Ralph Waldo Emerson

99

DAY TWO

Faithfulness! The bible says, "To whom much is given, much is required". Did you know that if you got EVERYTHING you asked for that you would have to work so much harder to maintain or gain more? NOTHING comes without a price! Consequences happen with every sequence (or action). If you are faithful over a few things then God will cause you to be established with many things. So be faithful where you are, over what you already have, and with who you are with.

#Godhonorsfaithfulness
#harvestisontheway

PRAYER:

Father God, thank You for Your faithfulness towards me. Thank You for all of Your blessings and mercy towards me. Help me to be faithful over all that You have committed to my hands and life. This I pray in Jesus' name. Amen.

SCRIPTURE:

Lamentations 3:22-23
Matthew 25:16-23
Luke 12:48

My Reflections and Revelations

_____

_____

_____

_____

_____

_____

_____

_____

_____

_____

_____

_____

_____

_____

_____

_____

_____

_____

_____

_____

"

"Always bear in mind that your own resolution to succeed is more important than any other thing." —*Abraham Lincoln*

"

DAY THREE

Change! Real Change requires planned efforts and consistency, along with a desire. Change your attitude about change and it will happen. A desire to change without an action plan is futile and a set up for failure! You wonder why you keep encountering the same challenges all of the time, it is because you have no plan in place! WRITE THE VISION; MAKE IT PLAIN; READ IT; AND RUN TO IT! You can lose the weight! You can build a successful thriving business! You can have a great marriage and successful family! Change can and will happen when YOU decide to maintain a desire, consistency, and a plan!

#letsdothis

PRAYER:

Father God, forgive me for doubting Your ability to change my life and circumstances if I put my trust in you and Your Word. Lord, I am willing to change, and I will commit to renewing my mind so that change can happen for me. Help me along the way to seek Your guidance before I make a move? I trust you and I know that You already have a plan for my life. Help me to accept Your plan and not doubt. This I pray in Jesus' name, Amen.

SCRIPTURE:

II Corinthians 5:17
Romans 12:2
Psalm 51:10

My Reflections and Revelations

_____
_____
_____
_____
_____
_____
_____
_____
_____
_____
_____
_____
_____
_____
_____
_____
_____
_____
_____
_____

"

"The one thing that lies at the foundation of positive change, the way I see it, is service to a fellow human being." -Lee Iacocca

"

DAY FOUR

Quiet time is essential for spiritual, mental and physical renewal. Every day is filled with activities that can and will drain you from every aspect of your being. It is to your benefit that you find time in your day to sit quietly; meditate on the Word; and revive your soul (mind, will and emotion). Without refueling you will encounter emptiness, a void that you cannot explain. At that point, you are vulnerable for other spirits to fill you up. Don't take that chance! Refuel daily!

> #befilledwiththeHolySpirit
> #walkinthelight

PRAYER:

Father God, forgive me for not seeking You daily for direction and refreshing. Examine me and help me to see anything in my life that is obstructing and preventing my relationship with You from becoming stronger. Fill me up with your Spirit so that I can properly represent Your love and Kingdom. Rescue me from my inner me that desires fulfillment of the flesh. This I pray in Jesus' name, Amen.

SCRIPTURES:

> Matthew 6:33
> Psalm 26:2
> Psalm 139:23

My Reflections and Revelations

_____
_____
_____
_____
_____
_____
_____
_____
_____
_____
_____
_____
_____
_____
_____
_____
_____
_____

66

"In every day, there are 1,440 minutes. That means we have 1,440 daily opportunities to make a positive impact" -Les Brown

99

DAY FIVE

Stuff happens! Things happen! IT Happened! Don't be afraid to start again. MOVE FORWARD! Forget what's behind, at least the feelings the event fostered, but not the lesson. STAND TALL! Dust yourself off and press full steam ahead. Block out negative voices or emotions. Set Chaos in order! NOW SHINE! God's FAVOR is with you!!

> #Godknowsyourname
> #Godhearsyourprayers
> #listenforHisvoice

PRAYER:

Father God, thank You that in the midst of my shortcomings, You know my name. Thank You for listening and hearing my prayers. When trouble is all about me I know that I can run to You for answers and comfort. I want to thank You Lord for being a strong tower and a refuge for me. I know that I can start again and be successful because of Your undying love. In Jesus' name I pray, Amen.

SCRIPTURE:

> Psalm 3:3
> Philippians 3:13
> Hebrews 4:16

My Reflections and Revelations

_____

_____

_____

_____

_____

_____

_____

_____

_____

_____

_____

_____

_____

_____

_____

_____

_____

_____

_____

_____

_____

66

*"Every next level of your life will demand
a different you!"—Unknown*

99

DAY SIX

Your journey to the top will come with victories, setbacks, disappointments, improvements, losses and gains. Sometimes the road or territory will be filled with sand, rocks, and gravel. You won't know what your next step will be. At those times, put on the FULL ARMOR of God, and PRESS your way FORWARD! Knowing that the battle is not yours, but it belongs to the Lord! Don't doubt the path that God has placed you on, even if you have to travel it alone.

> #thesebootsaremadeforwalking
> #stepsorderedbyGod
> #heisawaymaker

PRAYER:

Father God, please help me to remember that I am never alone, and even when times are hard You are a constant presence to help me to endure, breakthrough, and succeed. Forgive me for doubting that You are able to bring me out of any situations I may encounter. Give me the strength that I need to press forward towards Your purpose and my destiny. In Jesus' name I pray, Amen.

SCRIPTURE:

> Psalm 37:23
> Psalm 46:1
> Philippians 1:6
> Philippians 4:9

My Reflections and Revelations

_____

_____

_____

_____

_____

_____

_____

_____

_____

_____

_____

_____

_____

_____

_____

_____

_____

_____

_____

66 ———————————————————————————————

*"Never bend your head. Always hold it high. Look
the world straight in the eye." –Helen Keller*

—————————————————————————————— 99

DAY SEVEN

Since Jesus is your example, be ENCOURAGED!! When it looked like it was ALL over, He died! They buried Him, but then He ROSE! Just because something in your life looks like it is over, it is really just the BEGINNING of your true purpose! Don't get stuck! REFOCUS! REFUEL! RISE UP AND SHINE! The only way UP is DOWN! When you get down that is when you realize that there is only "up from here".

#RiseandmoveFORWARD

PRAYER:

Father God, thank You for allowing Jesus to die for my sins, and for being an example of Your power, love, and goodness. Help me to remember not only who I am, but also whose I am, so that I can look up and live. Thank You for Your Spirit and Word that keeps me headed in the right direction. Help me to remember what You have already done for me so that I can embrace my future. In Jesus' name I pray, Amen.

SCRIPTURE:

Deuteronomy 8:18
Psalms 91:15
Psalm 118:6

My Reflections and Revelations

_____
_____
_____
_____
_____
_____
_____
_____
_____
_____
_____
_____
_____
_____
_____
_____
_____
_____

66

"What you get by achieving your goals is not as important as what you become by achieving your goals." –Zig Ziglar

99

DAY EIGHT

I QUIT!! Oh how wonderfully easy that would be! Just sit around and do nothing ALL day, All week, All month, All year! Wait…what would that accomplish? An old saying is that "nothing from nothing yields nothing". Therefore, my children, you MUST make EVERYDAY count! Nothing that you do or attempt to do is wasted. There is an ethic to hard work. It ALWAYS produces success in some form or another. Don't Quit! Don't throw in the towel! Don't walk away; your labor is not in vain. Don't get weary in doing what's right and good because a windfall of blessings is happening and you need to see it come to pass! Don't faint!

> #Keepitmoving #noturningback #youaregood
> #youaresuccessful #youareimportant

PRAYER:

Father God, forgive me for not believing in my life's purpose. Help me to stand through hard times. I will not quit, but will push forward to completion, so that I can be a godly example to those who are watching my life. I want to thank You Lord for endurance. In Jesus' name I pray, Amen!

SCRIPTURE:

> Psalm 39:4
> James 4:14
> Philippians 1:6

My Reflections and Revelations

_____
_____
_____
_____
_____
_____
_____
_____
_____
_____
_____
_____
_____
_____
_____
_____
_____
_____
_____
_____

66 ————————————————————————————

*"Faith doesn't make sense, but it does make
MIRACLES!" –Prophet Robert Charles Blakes Sr.*

——————————————————————————— 99

DAY NINE

In your pursuit of "Happiness" and success don't abuse, neglect or forget about the very things or people that bring you joy! It is easy to allow the pressures of this world and all of its challenges to cause us to lose sight of what is REALLY important! Don't make big decisions when you are tired, hungry, or angry. Step back, Retreat, and Re-evaluate! Listen for God's voice and if you have to move on, just know that if no one else is with you, HE is!

> #TrustGod
> #Keepitmoving
> #Youwillbeokay
> #GreaterisHe

PRAYER:

Father God, thank You for going before, keeping and guiding me throughout my life. Help me to continue to listen for Your voice and instructions in my daily walk in this life. Help me to help others to desire a relationship with You, even as my own is strengthened. In Jesus' name I pray, Amen.

SCRIPTURE:

> Deuteronomy 31:8
> Isaiah 41:10
> John 16:33

My Reflections and Revelations

"

"When you have a dream, you've got to grab it and never let go" —Carol Burnett

"

CONCLUSION

I just want each one of you to know that my love for you is not conditional and that there is NOTHING that you can do to stop me from always loving you. I pray fervently for each of you daily. I am your history, but you are my future…And because of you, my future is bright! Parents fulfill their dreams through their children. I see Entrepreneurs, Educators, Organizers, Financiers and sheer talent that cannot be taught but is innate. All of the things that I dreamed of, I see in you! Thank you for being so talented focused, driven, and dedicated to KEEPING THE DREAM ALIVE! I cannot imagine what the next generation will bring to our legacy.

> #staystrong
> #stayfocused
> #stayconnectedtoGodandeachother
> #ancestorsareproud

DAILY SCRIPTURE REFERENCES

All scripture quoted directly from King James Version of Holy Bible

Day One

Mark 11:24

Therefore I say unto you, what things soever ye desire, when ye pray, believe that ye receive them, and ye shall have them.

Philippians 4:13

I can do all things through Christ which strengtheneth me.

John 14:18

I will not leave you comfortless: I will come to you.

Day Two

1 John 4:4

Ye are of God, little children, and have overcome them: because greater is he that is in you, than he that is in the world.

Deuteronomy 31:8

And the LORD, he it is that doth go before thee; he will be with thee, he will not fail thee, neither forsake thee: fear not, neither be dismayed.

Matthew 6:33

But seek ye first the kingdom of God, and his righteousness; and all these things shall be added unto you.

Day Three

Lamentations 3:22-23

It is of the LORD's mercies that we are not consumed, because his compassions fail not.

They are new every morning: great is thy faithfulness.

Psalm 139:14

I will praise thee; for I am fearfully and wonderfully made: marvelous are thy works; and that my soul knoweth right well.

Psalm 119:77

Let thy tender mercies come unto me, that I may live: for thy law is my delight.

Day Four

Psalm 103:4

Who redeemeth thy life from destruction; who crowneth thee with lovingkindness and tender mercies;

Deuteronomy 31:8

And the LORD, he it is that doth go before thee; he will be with thee, he will not fail thee, neither forsake thee: fear not, neither be dismayed.

Romans 8:37

Nay, in all these things we are more than conquerors through him that loved us.

Day Five

Philippians 4:13

I can do all things through Christ which strengtheneth me.

Ephesians 6:11

Put on the whole armour of God, that ye may be able to stand against the wiles of the devil."

Proverbs 3:6

In all thy ways acknowledge him, and he shall direct thy paths.

Day Six

Proverbs 9:10

The fear of the LORD is the beginning of wisdom: and the knowledge of the holy is understanding.

Philippians 4:13

I can do all things through Christ which strengtheneth me.

Philippians 2:5

Let this mind be in you, which was also in Christ Jesus:

Day Seven

Proverbs 3:4-5

So shalt thou find favour and good understanding in the sight of God and man. Trust in the LORD with all thine heart; and lean not unto thine own understanding.

John 14:16

And I will pray the Father, and he shall give you another Comforter, that he may abide with you forever;

Psalm 55:17

Evening, and morning, and at noon, will I pray, and cry aloud: and he shall hear my voice.

Day Eight

Philippians 1:6

Being confident of this very thing, that he which hath begun a good work in you will perform it until the day of Jesus Christ:

Ecclesiastics 9:11

I returned, and saw under the sun, that the race is not to the swift, nor the battle to the strong, neither yet bread to the wise, nor yet riches to men of understanding, nor yet favour to men of skill; but time and chance happeneth to them all.

Proverbs 3:5

Trust in the LORD with all thine heart; and lean not unto thine own understanding.

Day Nine

Psalm 29:11

The LORD will give strength unto his people; the LORD will bless his people with peace.

Jeremiah 29:11

For I know the thoughts that I think toward you, saith the LORD, thoughts of peace, and not of evil, to give you an expected end.

Philippians 4:7

And the peace of God, which passeth all understanding, shall keep your hearts and minds through Christ Jesus.

Day Ten

Hebrews 12:2

Looking unto Jesus the author and finisher of our faith; who for the joy that was set before him endured the cross, despising the shame, and is set down at the right hand of the throne of God.

Habakkuk 2:2

And the LORD answered me, and said, Write the vision, and make it plain upon tables, that he may run that readeth it.

I John 4:4

Ye are of God, little children, and have overcome them: because greater is he that is in you, than he that is in the world.

Day Eleven

Genesis 1:26-28

And God said, Let us make man in our image, after our likeness: and let them have dominion over the fish of the sea, and over the fowl of the air, and over the cattle, and over all the earth, and over every creeping thing that creepeth upon the earth.

So God created man in his own image, in the image of God created he him; male and female created he them.

And God blessed them, and God said unto them, Be fruitful, and multiply, and replenish the earth, and subdue it: and have dominion over the fish of the sea, and over the fowl of the air, and over every living thing that moveth upon the earth.

Mark 9:24

And straightway the father of the child cried out, and said with tears, Lord, I believe; help thou mine unbelief.

Romans 8:28

And we know that all things work together for good to them that love God, to them who are the called according to his purpose.

Day Twelve

John 16:33

These things I have spoken unto you, that in me ye might have peace. In the world ye shall have tribulation: but be of good cheer; I have overcome the world.

Psalm 121:1-2

I will lift up mine eyes unto the hills, from whence cometh my help.

My help cometh from the LORD, which made heaven and earth.

Isaiah 45:2

I will go before thee, and make the crooked places straight: I will break in pieces the gates of brass, and cut in sunder the bars of iron:

Day Thirteen

Ephesians 6:11-18

Put on the whole armour of God, that ye may be able to stand against the wiles of the devil.

For we wrestle not against flesh and blood, but against principalities, against powers, against the rulers of the darkness of this world, against spiritual wickedness in high places.

Wherefore take unto you the whole armour of God, that ye may be able to withstand in the evil day, and having done all, to stand.

Stand therefore, having your loins girt about with truth, and having on the breastplate of righteousness;

And your feet shod with the preparation of the gospel of peace;

Above all, taking the shield of faith, wherewith ye shall be able to quench all the fiery darts of the wicked.

And take the helmet of salvation, and the sword of the Spirit, which is the word of God:

Praying always with all prayer and supplication in the Spirit, and watching thereunto with all perseverance and supplication for all saints;

Isaiah 54:17

No weapon that is formed against thee shall prosper; and every tongue that shall rise against thee in judgment thou shalt condemn. This is the heritage of the servants of the LORD, and their righteousness is of me, saith the LORD.

John 1:5

And the light shineth in darkness; and the darkness comprehended it not.

Day Fourteen

Ephesians 3:20

Now unto him that is able to do exceeding abundantly above all that we ask or think, according to the power that worketh in us,

Proverbs 18:21

Death and life are in the power of the tongue: and they that love it shall eat the fruit thereof.

Psalm 19:14

Let the words of my mouth, and the meditation of my heart, be acceptable in thy sight, O LORD, my strength, and my redeemer.

Day Fifteen

Proverbs 6:2

Thou art snared with the words of thy mouth, thou art taken with the words of thy mouth.

Romans 4:17

(As it is written, I have made thee a father of many nations,) before him whom he believed, even God, who quickeneth the dead, and calleth those things which be not as though they were.

Psalm 10:14

Thou hast seen it; for thou beholdest mischief and spite, to requite it with thy hand: the poor committeth himself unto thee; thou art the helper of the fatherless.

Day Sixteen

Nehemiah 8:10

Then he said unto them, Go your way, eat the fat, and drink the sweet, and send portions unto them for whom nothing is prepared: for this day is holy unto our LORD: neither be ye sorry; for the joy of the LORD is your strength.

Matthew 6:33

But seek ye first the kingdom of God, and his righteousness; and all these things shall be added unto you.

Acts 17:28

For in him we live, and move, and have our being; as certain also of your own poets have said, for we are also his offspring.

Day Seventeen

Matthew 6:33

But seek ye first the kingdom of God, and his righteousness; and all these things shall be added unto you.

Matthew 25:23

His lord said unto him, Well done, good and faithful servant; thou hast been faithful over a few things, I will make thee ruler over many things: enter thou into the joy of thy lord.

James 1:23

For if any be a hearer of the word, and not a doer, he is like unto a man beholding his natural face in a glass:

Day Eighteen

Phil 4:8

Finally, brethren, whatsoever things are true, whatsoever things are honest, whatsoever things are pure, whatsoever things are lovely, whatsoever things are of good report; if there be any virtue, and if there be any praise, think on these things.

Proverbs 3:5-6

Trust in the LORD with all thine heart; and lean not unto thine own understanding.

In all thy ways acknowledge him, and he shall direct thy paths.

Zechariah 4:6

Then he answered and spake unto me, saying, This is the word of the LORD unto Zerubbabel, saying, not by might, nor by power, but by my spirit, saith the LORD of hosts.

Day Nineteen

Ecclesiastes 3:11

He hath made everything beautiful in his time: also he hath set the world in their heart, so that no man can find out the work that God maketh from the beginning to the end.

II Corinthians 6:2

(For he saith, I have heard thee in a time accepted, and in the day of salvation have I succoured thee: behold, now is the accepted time; behold, now is the day of salvation.)

Psalm 90:12

So teach us to number our days, that we may apply our hearts unto wisdom.

Day Twenty

I Peter 5:7

Casting all your care upon him; for he careth for you.

Isaiah 41:13

For I the LORD thy God will hold thy right hand, saying unto thee, Fear not; I will help thee.

Psalm 27:1

The LORD is my light and my salvation; whom shall I fear? The LORD is the strength of my life; of whom shall I be afraid?

Day Twenty-One

Hebrews 4:16

Let us therefore come boldly unto the throne of grace, that we may obtain mercy, and find grace to help in time of need.

Proverbs 16:3

Commit thy works unto the LORD, and thy thoughts shall be established.

Psalm 143:8

Cause me to hear thy lovingkindness in the morning; for in thee do I trust: cause me to know the way wherein I should walk; for I lift up my soul unto thee.

Day Twenty-Two

I John 5:14

And this is the confidence that we have in him, that, if we ask any thing according to his will, he heareth us:

Psalm 62:7

In God is my salvation and my glory: the rock of my strength, and my refuge, is in God.

Psalm 145:18

The LORD is nigh unto all them that call upon him, to all that call upon him in truth.

Day Twenty-Three

Proverbs 16:20

He that handleth a matter wisely shall find good: and whoso trusteth in the LORD, happy is he.

Psalm 31:19

Oh how great is thy goodness, which thou hast laid up for them that fear thee; which thou hast wrought for them that trust in thee before the sons of men!

James 1:5

If any of you lack wisdom, let him ask of God, that giveth to all men liberally, and upbraideth not; and it shall be given him.

Day Twenty-Four

Acts 17:27

That they should seek the Lord, if haply they might feel after him, and find him, though he be not far from every one of us:

Hebrews 11:6

But without faith it is impossible to please him: for he that cometh to God must believe that he is, and that he is a rewarder of them that diligently seek him.

James 4:8

Draw nigh to God, and he will draw nigh to you. Cleanse your hands, ye sinners; and purify your hearts, ye double minded.

Day Twenty-Five

Lamentations 3:22-23

It is of the Lord's mercies that we are not consumed, because his compassions fail not.

They are new every morning: great is thy faithfulness.

Hebrews 13:8

Jesus Christ the same yesterday, and today, and forever.

Philippians 4:19

But my God shall supply all your need according to his riches in glory by Christ Jesus.

Day Twenty-Six

Psalm 103:1

Bless the Lord, O my soul: and all that is within me, bless his holy name.

Psalm 16:11

Thou wilt shew me the path of life: in thy presence is fullness of joy; at thy right hand there are pleasures for evermore.

John 4:24

God is a Spirit: and they that worship him must worship him in spirit and in truth.

Day Twenty-Seven

Genesis 18:14

Is anything too hard for the LORD? At the time appointed I will return unto thee, according to the time of life, and Sarah shall have a son.

Isaiah 41:10

Fear thou not; for I am with thee: be not dismayed; for I am thy God: I will strengthen thee; yea, I will help thee; yea, I will uphold thee with the right hand of my righteousness.

Jeremiah 29:11

For I know the thoughts that I think toward you, saith the LORD, thoughts of peace, and not of evil, to give you an expected end.

Day Twenty-Eight

Jeremiah 33:3

Call unto me, and I will answer thee, and show thee great and mighty things, which thou knowest not.

Proverbs 3:5

Trust in the LORD with all thine heart; and lean not unto thine own understanding.

Hebrews 4:16

Let us therefore come boldly unto the throne of grace, that we may obtain mercy, and find grace to help in time of need.

Day Twenty-Nine

Matthew 5:16

Let your light so shine before men, that they may see your good works, and glorify your Father which is in heaven.

Ephesians 2:10

For we are his workmanship, created in Christ Jesus unto good works, which God hath before ordained that we should walk in them.

Deuteronomy 11:1

Therefore thou shalt love the LORD thy God, and keep his charge, and his statutes, and his judgments, and his commandments, alway.

Day Thirty

Isaiah 55:6

Seek ye the LORD while he may be found, call ye upon him while he is near:

Matthew 27:51

And, behold, the veil of the temple was rent in twain from the top to the bottom; and the earth did quake, and the rocks rent;

Hebrews 4:16

Let us therefore come boldly unto the throne of grace, that we may obtain mercy, and find grace to help in time of need.

Day Thirty-One

Psalm 119:105

Thy word is a lamp unto my feet, and a light unto my path.

Proverbs 3:6-7

In all thy ways acknowledge him, and he shall direct thy paths.

Be not wise in thine own eyes: fear the LORD, AND DEPART FROM EVIL.

I Kings 19:12

And after the earthquake a fire; but the LORD was not in the fire: and after the fire a still small voice.

BONUS DAYS

Day One

Deuteronomy 28:3-5

Blessed shalt thou be in the city, and blessed shalt thou be in the field.

Blessed shall be the fruit of thy body, and the fruit of thy ground, and the fruit of thy cattle, the increase of thy kine, and the flocks of thy sheep.

Blessed shall be thy basket and thy store

Proverbs 16:3

Commit thy works unto the LORD, and thy thoughts shall be established.

John 10:10

The thief cometh not, but for to steal, and to kill, and to destroy: I am come that they might have life, and that they might have it more abundantly.

Day Two

Lamentations 3:22-23

It is of the LORD's mercies that we are not consumed, because his compassions fail not.

They are new every morning: great is thy faithfulness.

Matthew 25:16:23

Then he that had received the five talents went and traded with the same, and made them other five talents.

And likewise he that had received two, he also gained other two.

But he that had received one went and digged in the earth, and hid his lord's money.

After a long time the lord of those servants cometh, and reckoneth with them.

And so he that had received five talents came and brought other five talents, saying, Lord, thou deliveredst unto me five talents: behold, I have gained beside them five talents more.

His lord said unto him, Well done, thou good and faithful servant: thou hast been faithful over a few things, I will make thee ruler over many things: enter thou into the joy of thy lord.

He also that had received two talents came and said, Lord, thou deliveredst unto me two talents: behold, I have gained two other talents beside them.

His lord said unto him, Well done, good and faithful servant; thou hast been faithful over a few things, I will make thee ruler over many things: enter thou into the joy of thy lord.

Then he which had received the one talent came and said, Lord, I knew thee that thou art an hard man, reaping where thou hast not sown, and gathering where thou hast not strawed:

And I was afraid, and went and hid thy talent in the earth: lo, there thou hast that is thine

Luke 12:48

But he that knew not, and did commit things worthy of stripes, shall be beaten with few stripes. For unto whomsoever much is given, of him shall be much required: and to whom men have committed much, of him they will ask the more.

Day Three

II Corinthians 5:17

Therefore if any man be in Christ, he is a new creature: old things are passed away; behold, all things are become new.

Romans 12:2

And be not conformed to this world: but be ye transformed by the renewing of your mind, that ye may prove what is that good, and acceptable, and perfect, will of God.

Psalm 51:10

Create in me a clean heart, O God; and renew a right spirit within me.

Day Four

Matthew 6:33

But seek ye first the kingdom of God, and his righteousness; and all these things shall be added unto you.

Psalm 26:2

Examine me, O Lord, and prove me; try my reins and my heart.

Psalm 139:23

Search me, O God, and know my heart: try me, and know my thoughts:

Day Five

Psalm 3:3

But thou, O LORD, art a shield for me; my glory, and the lifter up of mine head.

Philippians 3:13

Brethren, I count not myself to have apprehended: but this one thing I do, forgetting those things which are behind, and reaching forth unto those things which are before,

Hebrews 4:16

Let us therefore come boldly unto the throne of grace, that we may obtain mercy, and find grace to help in time of need.

Day Six

Psalm 37:23

The steps of a good man are ordered by the LORD: and he delighteth in his way.

Psalm 46:1
God is our refuge and strength, a very present help in trouble.

Philippians 1:6

Being confident of this very thing, that he which hath begun a good work in you will perform it until the day of Jesus Christ:

Philippians 4:9

Those things, which ye have both learned, and received, and heard, and seen in me, do: and the God of peace shall be with you.

Day Seven

Deuteronomy 8:18

But thou shalt remember the Lord thy God: for it is he that giveth thee power to get wealth, that he may establish his covenant which he sware unto thy fathers, as it is this day.

Psalms 91:15

He shall call upon me, and I will answer him: I will be with him in trouble; I will deliver him, and honour him.

Psalm 118:6

The Lord is on my side; I will not fear: what can man do unto me?

Day Eight

Psalm 39:4

Lord, make me to know mine end, and the measure of my days, what it is: that I may know how frail I am.

James 4:14

Whereas ye know not what shall be on the morrow. For what is your life? It is even a vapour, that appeareth for a little time, and then vanisheth away.

Philippians 1:6

Being confident of this very thing, that he which hath begun a good work in you will perform it until the day of Jesus Christ:

Day Nine

Deuteronomy 31:8

And the Lord, he it is that doth go before thee; he will be with thee, he will not fail thee, neither forsake thee: fear not, neither be dismayed.

Isaiah 41:10

Fear thou not; for I am with thee: be not dismayed; for I am thy God: I will strengthen thee; yea, I will help thee; yea, I will uphold thee with the right hand of my righteousness.

John 16:33

These things I have spoken unto you, that in me ye might have peace. In the world ye shall have tribulation: but be of good cheer; I have overcome the world.

My Reflections and Revelations

_____
_____
_____
_____
_____
_____
_____
_____
_____
_____
_____
_____
_____
_____
_____
_____
_____
_____
_____
_____

““

"Perseverance is the hard work you do after you get tired of doing the hard work you already did" Newt Gingrich

””

My Reflections and Revelations

_____

_____

_____

_____

_____

_____

_____

_____

_____

_____

_____

_____

_____

_____

_____

_____

_____

_____

_____

❝

"Believe deep down in your heart that you are destined to do great things." –Joe Paterno

❞

My Reflections and Revelations

_____

_____

_____

_____

_____

_____

_____

_____

_____

_____

_____

_____

_____

_____

_____

_____

_____

_____

_____

_____

_____

_____

_____

"

"Problems are not stop signs, they are guidelines." —Robert Schuller

"

My Reflections and Revelations

‎

"

"*Optimism is a happiness magnet. If you stay positive, good things and good people will be drawn to you.*" *Mary Lou Retton*

"

My Reflections and Revelations

_____
_____
_____
_____
_____
_____
_____
_____
_____
_____
_____
_____
_____
_____
_____
_____
_____
_____
_____
_____

66 ——————————————————————————————

"Wherever you go, no matter what the weather, always bring your own sunshine." —Anthony J. D'Angelo

————————————————————————————— 99

My Reflections and Revelations

_____
_____
_____
_____
_____
_____
_____
_____
_____
_____
_____
_____
_____
_____
_____
_____
_____
_____
_____

66 ——————————————————————————

*"Arise, awake and stop not till the goal is
reached."-Swami Vivekananda*

—————————————————————————— 99

My Reflections and Revelations

_____
_____
_____
_____
_____
_____
_____
_____
_____
_____
_____
_____
_____
_____
_____
_____
_____
_____
_____
_____
_____

❝

"There are far, far better things ahead than anything we leave behind." —C.S. Lewis

❞

My Reflections and Revelations

" ――――――――――――――――――――――――

"The less you respond to negative people, the more
positive your life will become." —Paulo Coelho

―――――――――――――――――――――― **"**

My Reflections and Revelations

_____

_____

_____

_____

_____

_____

_____

_____

_____

_____

_____

_____

_____

_____

_____

_____

_____

_____

_____

66

"Get Ready! Get Ready! Get Ready! God is going to do the miraculous for you today!" —Bishop T.D. Jakes

99

My Reflections and Revelations

_____

_____

_____

_____

_____

_____

_____

_____

_____

_____

_____

_____

_____

_____

_____

_____

_____

_____

_____

_____

66 ————————————————————————

"Don't camouflage the real you to make others comfortable." —Maronda Chenault

———————————————————————— 99

My Reflections and Revelations

My Reflections and Revelations

_____
_____
_____
_____
_____
_____
_____
_____
_____
_____
_____
_____
_____
_____
_____
_____
_____
_____
_____

"

"Dwell on the beauty of life. Watch the stars, and see yourself running with them." —Marcus Aurelius

"

Contact Information
Joyace G. Ussin
Clarioncallwm1@yahoo.com
Joyaceussin@yahoo.com
Facebook: Joyace G. Ussin
Twitter: @joyaceussin
713-471-7004

CPSIA information can be obtained
at www.ICGtesting.com
Printed in the USA
BVHW030346221119
564501BV00001B/173/P

9 781973 676096